Italian
Gardens

Judith Wade

Italian
Gardens

RIZZOLI
NEW YORK

Grandi Giardini Italiani/Great Italian Gardens
Piazza Cavour, 6, 22060 Cabiate (Como)
Tel. 031-756211/756769 fax 031-756768
e-mail grandigiardini@tiscalinet.it web site www.grandigiardini.it

Great Italian Gardens is an organization dedicated to educating the public about the rich artistic and botanical heritage of Italian gardens.

The author would like to thank the owners of the gardens, their gardeners, and especially Mimma Pallavicini, Lorena Lombroso, Maria Angela Gropallo, and Carlotta for their help in compiling this book.

Editing: Roberta Garbarini
Graphic design: Sottsass Associati, Mario Milizia, and Monica Lovati
Layout: Antonietta Pietrobon

First published in the United States of America in 2002 by
Rizzoli International Publications, Inc.
300 Park Avenue South
New York, NY 10010

© 2002 by Rizzoli Libri Illustrati
Società Editoria Artistica SpA
Gruppo Skira
© 2002 Judith Wade (Great Italian Gardens) for the texts and photographs,
except for the photographs by Massimo Listri

2002 2003 2004 2005 2006 / 10 9 8 7 6 5 4 3 2 1

Library of Congress Control Number: 2002106884

ISBN: 0-8478-2495-0

Printed in Italy

Page 2: the tree lined avenue at Villa Manzoni at Brusuglio; pg. 6–7: the lush and exotic vegetation at Villa Tritone at Sorrento; pg. 8–9: nature and artifice at Villa del Balbianello on Lake Como.

Contents

Preface

"Our bodies are our gardens, to the which our wills are gardeners."
Shakespeare, *Othello* I, iii

From north to south, from the Adriatic to the Tyrrhenian, *Italian Gardens* takes the reader on a journey through some of the most beautiful gardens in Italy. It features gardens which represent more than five hundred years of Italian garden design, from those which epitomize the sublime rigor of the Italian parterre to those which incorporate whimsical and surreal decorative motifs. Thirty-seven gardens are included from eleven Italian regions.

Without living it personally, without smelling it or seeing it with one's own eyes, it is impossible to describe the scent of a thousand roses in bloom at Palazzo Patrizi, or the intoxicating fragrance of the lavenders which are spread out on the fields like a purple cloud at Villa Pasolini Dall'Onda. It is difficult, too, to describe the stunning effect of the many colors used by the important contemporary garden designer Russell Page at San Liberato. One will revel in the vestiges of the past which these gardens maintain, elements which remind us that the garden was a place of privilege for leisure and entertainment such as the charming outdoor theater carved from the greenery at Villa Geggiano. Other reminders of the past abound as well, including traces of ancient gardening trades. They are preserved in the little agricultural museum at Palazzo Fantini at Tredozio, while at the annual Exhibition of the Artisan at the Corsini al Prato garden in Florence one can still find artisans who are able to restore an antique wrought iron gate or repair an ancient terra-cotta pot.

Water is an important element in these gardens, whether it functions as a decorative element or as an essential part of sustaining the garden. And of course many of the gardens overlook bodies of water, such as Lake Como which borders Villa Balbinello and Villa Monastero, or the Lake of Lugano at the foot of the glorious Villa Favorita. The sea heightens the impression of the box parterre at the Cervara Abbey at San Girolamo on the Hill of Portofino. The Bay of Sorrento enhances the scene of the tropical garden at Villa Tritone and the Gulf of La Spezia hugs the Villa Marigola and its parterre.

Many of the gardens featured have great historical import such as the Isola Bella, the Giusti Garden, Villa Cicogna Mozzoni, and Villa Garzoni; they should be thought of as open-air museums that preserve hundreds of years of artistic and botanical history. Interest in maintaining these "museums" has grown considerably over the years as the public has become aware of the plight of gardens which are in jeopardy because of urban and suburban development. The FAI, Fondo per l'Ambiente Italiano (Italian

Environment Fund), has been working for years on the maintenance of its gardens which are in its care and has made a considerable positive impact on the longevity of these places. A great deal of civic sense is required to open the gates to visitors, but the Italian public is passionate about gardens, and they are able to respect the environment and the value of these extraordinary places. And indeed the owners and custodians of the gardens featured within are responsible for their continued existence as well. In some cases, these gardens have belonged to the same family for hundreds of years. These dedicated caretakers have made the public aware of the gardens and their importance.

The last gardens discussed in the book are from southern Italy. The dry climate has posed some challenges but the results of the efforts are remarkable. Miki Borghese, owner of Il Biviere, has reclaimed a dried up lake to make it the kingdom of the best succulents and Mediterranean plants. In Ischia another "miracle": a stone quarry has been stubbornly transformed into a botanical paradise. Susana Walton, owner of La Mortella, has shown that even in the south, and even in a corner of an island ignored by institutions, one of the most beautiful gardens in Europe can be created and maintained. Maybe, as Susana Walton says, one has to be a little mad to dedicate one's heart and soul to a garden. That is, if "mad" means a person who has a passion and an extraordinary respect for those places that are often forgotten. Fortunately, there are, in Italy and around the world, increasing numbers of people who are "mad" for the beauty and history within the landscape.

This book, therefore, speaks first and foremost to those who love the land. The owners and curators have expressed this sentiment in the form of a garden. *Italian Gardens* is my way of paying my homage to those magnificent—and beneficent—sentiments.

Judith Wade

Introduction

by Maria Brambilla

Thirty-seven gardens have been chosen as examples of great Italian gardens. They are different in age, size, and characteristics, but it is for this reason that they offer a complete picture of the natural decorative greenery scattered in every corner of Italy.

Some of them have an imposing history because they are hundreds of years old. There are gardens that have succumbed to the inevitable changes wrought by the passing years. And some owners required their gardens to be reshaped according to the various fashions, styles, and tastes of the times. But they were also able to preserve many traces of the gardens' illustrious pasts, such as geometrical parterres, informal parks, botanical collections, statuary, lemon orchards, and open-air theaters sculpted in the vegetation. This variety of elements—and the ways in which they were achieved in different eras—makes this journey through the art of the Italian garden a fascinating one.

The flat surfaces sustained by robust walls that can be admired in the Garzoni garden or in that of Vignanello, are testimony to a technique that was much admired in the Renaissance. The idea of excavating the hillside to obtain a tier of broad steps was certainly much older. But it was Italian Renaissance architects, from Michelozzo to Bramante and Pirro Ligorio, who deserve credit for using this agricultural technique for the cultivation of gardens, later adopted all over the world.

Many great gardens of the past have renewed the style of the Italian garden, with box hedges tidily pruned in topiary shapes. This is the terrace of Castello di Vignanello, leaning against the strong walls that were created to correct the uneven hillside.

The parterre is also a frequent feature of the great Italian gardens. This was another spectacular invention of Renaissance gardeners. They were refined furnishings spread at the feet of the palazzos like carpets, decorated with low borders of perfectly manicured (sculpted) evergreen plants used to design flower beds, spirals, scrolls, family initials, and family crests. These spaces were not designed to be crossed on foot. (For strolls in the garden there were the shady avenues with pergolas covered with climbing plants). Rather, they were there to beautify the view for the owners of the house. For this reason, the design of these gardens can only be appreciated from the windows of the second floor, the *piano nobile* of a Renaissance palazzo. The parterre has also taken its place in the formal gardens seen in succeeding centuries and all over Europe, particularly in seventeenth-century France. Supple hedges of box were used like embroidery threads to make ever more elaborate patterns in the shape of arabesques, vine branches, and feathers. These patterns were then filled in with flowers or colored sand.

For elements dating back to the dawn of the Italian garden, there are also the vases of citrus placed at regular intervals along the borders of the avenues and the flower beds. For centuries they have been considered the most precious, romantic, and indispensable garden decoration, with their shiny evergreen leaves, their headily scented flowers, and their sun-colored fruit. They were a reference to the mythical Golden Age, but they were also a testimony to the ability of the gardeners and, by reflection, the owners. In Tuscany and Lombardy, the difficult challenge to nature was to have these citrus plants survive in a place where winters were cold. In order to achieve this, the plants were cultivated in classic large terra-cotta

Statues and man made decorations play as important a role in the Italian garden as do the plants. The rare and valuable statues actually form an out-door museum and add to the historical and artistic interest of the garden.

vases that could be sheltered indoors during the winter. In these shelters, which were great walled rooms with large windows, the vases were placed with great botanical expertise and following precise rules: the citron trees (*Citrus medica*) were placed in front of the windows because it was thought that they needed more sun; in the second row came the oranges; and next to the wall were the lemons. A perfect example can be admired in the garden at Villa Grabau, where they are perfectly preserved.

The statues were even more highly prized. They were used in a variety of ways: they were placed on the balustrades that enclosed the terraced areas; they were mounted in recesses cut out of the vegetation; or they were set on pedestals that punctuated the borders of the avenues. They were works of art but they were also a means of communication. Aside from serving as representations of various allegorical stories, they indicated to the visitors and guests the refinement and wealth of the owners of the house. The wealthier owners, like the powerful cardinals of the sixteenth century, would buy pieces brought to light by the first archeological excavations. In their gardens they could show off genuine collections of antiques. Those who did not have access to these treasures would commission sculptures and other figures in stone from the best artist of the period. Nowadays, seeing the statues that for centuries had populated the formal gardens is a rarity. Many have been lost and others have been taken to safety in houses or museums; only a few stand at their posts defying theft and the weather.

However, the most important characteristic of the Italian garden is the sculpting of plants according to the art of topiary. This technique was developed in ancient Rome where, to beautify those parts of the garden that were most in view. The branches of holm oaks, laurel, box, cypresses, myrtle, and other evergreens were pruned and bent to obtain different shapes. Spheres, cones, pyramids, and also human figures in their divine or mortal forms were created. The art of topiary was then rediscovered by Renaissance architects. They used the green sculptures to show off man's ability to tame nature—to control its untidy exuberance—and to make the garden a place of order and harmony. The sculptures were also used to make the garden a place of artifice—of show and illusion—as we see from the green outdoor theaters that are preserved in some gardens like Grabau, Rizzardi, and Geggiano. This decoration was born out of the fusion between the kingdom of Nature and that of architecture, with a lawn that is transformed into a stage—espaliers of yew pruned into walls that form the wings and backdrop, and even the prompter's box or the conductor's podium cut out in box. These theaters were often a decorative element without any practical function. But they were sometimes used to put on shows performed by the owners of the house and their guests.

Later, during the nineteenth century, the fashion for landscaping that was born in England reached Italy. And so, alongside the parterres, the statues, the terra-cotta citrus vases, and the plants sculpted according to the rules of topiary, one finds rolling lawns, winding pathways, irregularly shaped lakes, and trees that change with the seasons. In some cases, the design of the old gardens was revolutionized to make room for new spaces where everything was supposed to seem natural and untamed by the hand of man. These were places where, in reality, there was very little of the spontaneous—every corner had been planned in details and with

Etching by Salomon Kleiner, 1738

Right. The garden at the Cervara Abbey in Santa Margherita Ligure is the only preserved Italian garden in Liguria.
The superb graduated cones in box make it even richer.

great attention and then kept under control by expert gardeners.

This great admiration for the English style of garden was accompanied by a passion for botany. Plants were imported from all over the world. Botanical collections took the place of antiques, and the gardens became a laboratory for the owners who experimented with the difficult task of cultivating exotic and unknown species. Alessandro Manzoni was among these enthusiasts. His love for exotic plants was matched by his curiosity for agricultural experiments. At Brusuglio, just outside Milan, Manzoni bred bees. He planted mulberry trees for the silk worms he imported from Japan. He lovingly cared for the hydrangea, magnolias, tulip trees, and catalpas that were still an absolute novelty in Lombardy at that time.

And last in the order of time, but not any less fascinating, are the younger gardens, those that are still not fifty years old and take on the most significant tendencies of contemporary landscaping. First among them are La Landriana, San Liberato, and La Mortella. These three green spaces were the design inventions of Russell Page, an Englishman, one of the great gardeners of the twentieth century. They are perfectly adapted to the colors and light of the Italian landscape. There are also gardens created by passionate proprietors which are beautiful in all the seasons and are must-sees because of the flowers, the scents, and the flashes of color. Indeed their precious natural heritages have been chosen and maintained with extraordinary care and devotion, and greatly deserve to be admired.

Water was a fundamental element of the great Italian gardens of the past. It was used to decorate Renaissance gardens, then as an element of surprise, as in the Garzoni garden at Collodi. It was transformed into a functional part of the landscape style of garden, and then into a vital resource for the contemporary Mediterranean gardens such as La Mortella in Ischia and La Landriana in Tor San Lorenzo.

Villa Favorita
Lugano

Villa Favorita and its garden are situated at the foot of the hill to Castagnola in Lugano. It is surely the most illustrious example of the aristocratic villa in the Ceresio area.

The story of the villa begins at the end of the seventeenth century, when Carlo Corrado Beroldingen decided to build his house here. In 1732 the villa and garden were bought by Giovanni Rodolfo Riva of Lugano. Another change of hands took place in 1919, when Prince Frederick Leopold of Prussia established his residence here. He is responsible for the beautiful avenue of cypresses that still leads to the villa gates. The villa passed into the hands of Baron Heinrich Thyssen-Bornemisza in 1932; he wanted a place where he could house his collection of paintings. Indeed, it was the baron who commissioned the art gallery, and he also restored many of the buildings and enlarged the garden. He was the father of the present owners.

The garden at Villa Favorita is similar to almost all the historical parks in the lakes area of Lombardy. They are often laid out parallel to the strand of the lake and not at right angles to the entrance to the building. The architectural plans also make use of hidden corners and terraces in order to create magic plays of light and shade to reflect the waters of the lake.

The waving tops of the cypress trees on one side and a dense growth of rhododendrons and other shrubs on the other embrace the orderly paved avenue that leads to Villa Favorita.

Apart from the stupendous cypresses, there is a great variety of plants to be seen. Among these are a Japanese cypress; a camphor tree; a tulip tree; some Ginkgo bilobas (maiden hair trees), which are considered to be sacred in China; magnolias; an *Osmanthus heterophyllus "Myrtifolius"*; privet; wisteria; rhododendron; camellias; roses; olive trees; and oleanders. In addition, there is a rare *Michelia soltsop* that was planted by the Dalai Lama during his visit to Villa Favorita in 1993. Since 1998 the grounds have been embellished by various collections of tree peonies and herbaceous perennials, Satzuki azaleas, lilies, and twenty-seven varieties of spreading camellias.

Above. The Lake of Lugano and its atmosphere can be seen through the cadenced lines of cypress. Right. The severity of the cypress trees is softened by a cushion of colorful irises that flower until the end of April.

Above. The different levels of vegetation in the garden both contrast and blend with the various shapes of the buildings of Villa Favorita and become an integral part of the architecture. Right. A number of antique statues, like this cherub, decorate and enhance the garden.

Parco della Villa Pallavicino
Stresa

The villa was built in 1862 for Ruggero Borghi, a friend of Alessandro Manzoni and Antonio Rosmini. A later owner, the Duke of Villambrosa, enlarged the villa and planted stands of trees such as tulip trees (*Lyriodendron tulipfera*) and sequoias that were almost unknown in Italy at the time.

The villa then passed into the hands of the Marchesi Pallavicino. The grounds were enriched with greenhouses and avenues, and the villa was beautified inside and out with new decorations, giving it the imposing style it has today.

The grounds cover approximately thirty-seven acres, and the property is situated in one of the most spectacular parts of Lake Maggiore. The vegetation is formed mostly of old chestnut trees, tulip trees, red beach, varieties of maple, larches, oaks, plane trees, magnolias, and majestic sequoias. A superb cedar of Lebanon competes in grandeur with the façade of the villa.

The main attraction of the grounds is the presence of more than fifty species of animals and birds. Kangaroos, zebra, deer, lama, and alpacas roam free. Swans glide in the lake with ducks, mallards, and other species of water birds. Various species of exotic parrots, toucans, calao (a black crow of Asian origin), and pheasant are bred in the beautiful aviaries. Ferrets, mongoose,

The rose garden at Villa Pallavicino flowers with colorful blooms throughout the summer. The majestic trees and the age-old greenhouses give the garden a fascinating serenity.

desert foxes, skunks, and other exotic animals live in perfectly acclimatized habitats.

The ancient stables are also open to the public. They have been partially transformed into a restaurant and a charming chalet that dominates the Italian garden and is decorated with brilliant flowers in every season. There is also a rose garden.

Above. View of Villa Pallavicino from the grounds. To the right of the façade can be seen the most magnificent examples of the cedars of Lebanon of Lake Maggiore.
Right. A glimpse of spring in the grounds, with azaleas and other spring flowers contrasting with the green of the trees. The mild climate of the lake brings an early spring flowering in March.

Left and above. Exotic animals and rare birds are an attraction of the park and an integral part of the gardens.
Right. The beds are planted with annuals and flowering bulbs. They renew the scenery at Villa Pallavicino with every change of season.

Isola Bella and Isola Madre
Verbania

In 1632 Count Vitaliano Borromeo began the construction of the monumental baroque palazzo and the majestic stage setting of the gardens. Today the gardens are a documentation of the splendors of an earlier age.

After a visit to the palazzo, where priceless works of art are on view in an elegant and sumptuous setting, visitors can take a walk in the garden. This classic and inimitable example of the seventeenth-century Italian garden is set out in decorated terraces laid one above the other. The spectacular flowers provide color and perfume from March to October.

A short boat ride away is Isola Madre. It is the largest of the Borromeo Islands and the most characteristic for its atmosphere of quiet, meditative enchantment. Peacocks, parrots, and pheasant roam free within the garden of rare plants and exotic flowers. Isola Madre is famous for its azaleas, rhododendrons, and camellias, but also for the old pergolas of wisteria, the largest example of Kashmir cypress in Europe, the espalier of oranges and lemons, the collection of hibiscus, and an admirable example of Ginkgo biloba.

In 1978 the sixteenth-century palazzo was opened to the public. Some of the rooms have been restored to their original splendor,

Rare trees and extraordinary shrubs make up the botanical collection at Isola Madre and are most appreciated at the change of the seasons, when the filtered light makes the landscape unforgettable.

and the palazzo is also famous for its collection of liveries, dolls, and porcelains. The exhibition of the Little Puppet Theatres dates back to the period of the seventeenth to nineteenth centuries.

One leaves Isola Madre remembering the refinement in the care of the gardens and the rooms, where the quality of the exhibitions is appreciated by the most demanding visitors.

Farther south, dominating the southern part of the lake, stands the Rocca Borromeo of Angera. This important construction, from which there is a beautiful panorama, bears the marks of the historical events of this land, with its traditions and centennial heritage. The whole expanse of the lake is crowned by the surrounding mountains of the Alps.

Above. Exotic birds can be found wandering in the garden at Isola Madre.
Right. A symphony of flowers against the sixteenth-century façade of the palazzo at Isola Madre. Bougainvillea and false jasmine combine with perennials and cannas in the border.

Above. The baroque splendor of the monumental garden at Isola Bella.
Right. Isola Bella's Italian garden is one of the most beautiful examples of this style. It is characterized by its grandeur and the contrast between the strict linearity of the curving beds and the changing patterns of the water on the lake that lies in the background.

Botanical Gardens of Villa Taranto, Verbania

Villa Taranto stands on the Piedmont side of Lake Maggiore between Intra and Pallanza. A Scottish captain, Neil McEacharn, bought the property from the Marquis of Sant'Elia in 1931 with the idea of creating a botanical garden of international repute. Creation of the garden started in 1936.

McEacharn was born in 1884 into a very rich, aristocratic Scottish family. This gave him the ability to dedicate his time to the great passions of his life—botany, gardening, and travel. He fell into the rare category of enthusiastic gentlemen who managed to go around the world many times (it seems that he did it seven times, the first time at the age of sixteen) looking for new plants to cultivate in their gardens at home.

Captain McEacharn admirably managed to match the botanical necessities of the residence with his aesthetic requirements. It was a beautiful site and the climate was mild. He set about the incredible job of excavating and terracing along Punta della Castagnola. His property consisted of forty-nine acres and included adjacent land which was purchased later. He created woods, borders, and avenues of shrubs, beds, parterres, lawns, lakes, and greenhouses. He planted specimens from all over the world, forming a very valuable scientific collection that today still

With its spectacular flowering bulbs, every corner of Villa Taranto sings the praises of spring in April.

numbers eighty-five hundred different species and varieties. Every year, more than 150,000 people visit.

McEacharn donated this jewel to the Italian State in 1938; it was opened to the public in 1952. McEacharn lived at Villa Taranto until he died in 1964. The English gardener, Henry Coker, was his associate.

April is the best time to visit because the more than eighty thousand bulbs are in flower and the garden takes on a brilliant, multicolored splendor. However, every season is of interest to the visitor: in the summer, the beds of annuals, aquatic plants, and later, more than three hundred varieties of dahlia are in bloom; in the fall, the color of the turning leaves is breathtaking.

Above. The parterre near the entrance flowers from spring to fall. The central column is an archeological find placed in the garden by Captain Mc Eacharn.
Right. The great heated greenhouses that contain lush, exotic plants. Some rare examples of Victoria regia *and* Victoria cruziana *reproduce in the water as they do in nature.*

La Cervara
Santa Margherita Ligure

La Cervara was once the vegetable garden of the Benedictine monastery of St. Girolamo al Deserto, founded in 1364. Today it is the only monumental Italian garden that has been preserved in Liguria.

The garden extends over two levels, gently joined together by pergolas and flights of steps. The upper part is characterized by octagonal pillars covered with *Trachelospermum jasminoides L.*, which gives off a delicious scent of jasmine when it is in flower. On the lower level, the box hedges *(Buxus sempervirens)* form geometrical shapes ornamented by graduated cones. They surround the seventeenth-century marble fountain with a figure of a cherub. In the summer, the basin of the fountain is colored by pink and white water lilies. In the western part of the lower garden there is a pepper tree *(Schimus mollis)* and toward the eastern part, a pergola covered by an enormous and old purple wisteria *(Wisteria sinesis L.)*. A eucalyptus *(Eucalyptus globolus)* stands behind the apse of the church, and the walls toward the abbey are covered with climbing fig *(Ficus repens)*, red capers, and cushions of blue bellflowers *(Campanula carpatica)*. There are also the very colorful birds of paradise *(strelizia)*, citrus plants, oleanders, and Aleppo pines.

The whole landscape complex of La Cervara was declared a national monument in 1912. The present owner has carried out a restoration

The lower level terrace at Cervara is the only Italian garden that has been conserved in Liguria. The geometric diamond shapes cut out in box culminate in the center in unusual graduated cones interspersed with spherical shapes.

project to conserve the original wooded area and the terraces on the side toward the mountain, and the garden toward the sea.

Important recuperative and restorative work was begun in 1990. The project was designed by the architect Mide Osculati. The restoration of the paintings was carried out by Pinin Brambilla Barcilon, who restored Leonardo da Vinci's *Last Supper*.

The strategic position of La Cervara, overlooking the sea between Santa Margherita Ligure and Portofino, makes the monumental complex a favorite place for concerts, weddings, and other events.

Above. A glimpse of the Italian garden looking toward the buildings – formal elements of exquisite elegance and flowering festoons.
Right. A view of the age-old wisteria that covers the pergola with its branches.

Left. The green of the vegetation contrasts beautifully with the restored cloister of the old abbey.
Right. The seventeenth-century fountain featuring a cherub appears among the spirals of box.

Villa Marigola
San Terenzo Lerici

The Cassa di Risparmio di La Spezia—a bank—is the owner of the villa. Since 1979, the bank has been improving the value of this architectural jewel and garden, which rise at the top of a promontory between the inlets of Lerici and San Terenzo. One of the most beautiful views of the Golfo dei Poeti (Gulf of Poets) can be seen from there. Villa Marigola fully synthesizes the typical style of the Ligurian "villa on the sea," and for more than two centuries it has fascinated its succeeding owners and their guests, as well as visitors. The first construction was built in the eighteenth century by the Marchesi Ollandini as a summer residence. The building was embellished by a terrace garden that faced the sea; the garden consisted of citrus fruits such as cedars, oranges, and bitter tangerines. Around the villa, slopes cultivated with vines and olives descended to the beach and the rocks. This littoral once included the "White House," its portico swept by the waves. The house was the last refuge of the English poet Percy Bysshe Shelley, and it was here that he was inspired to write *Lines Written in the Bay of Lerici*: "And the scent of winged flowers, / and the coolness of the hours / of dew, and sweet warmth left by day, / were scattered o'er the twinkling bay."

The eighteenth century saw the formation of the romantic park,

The terrace of the sea-facing façade of Villa Marigola was redesigned in 1926. It is another interpretation of the Italian garden. The lines have been softened and cascade into a mixture of citrus plants, palms, cypress, and other Mediterranean trees.

with paths that ended in natural open balconies overlooking the coastal landscape. The villa has always had a cultural vocation and hosted the Emperor of Germany, Frederick III, and the great symbolist painter Arnold Böcklin. An area of the park was even called "Böcklin's garden" in honor of the subjects of his works. The dramatist Sem Benelli, who wrote *La cena delle beffe* here, was also a longtime guest at Marigola.

The present appearance of Marigola dates back to 1926 when the property was bought by the ship owner and senator Giovanni Bibolini and the architect Franco Oliva, who executed the plans to enlarge the building. At this time, the sinuous geometrical patterns of the present Italian–style parterre were laid down, replacing the garden of citrus trees.

Above. The airy parterre leads the eye towards the Golfo dei Poeti (Gulf of Poets).
Right. The seascape is framed by the ilex in this garden. It was the inspiration of the many artists who had been guests at Villa Marigola over the years.

Villa Cicogna Mozzoni
Bisuschio

Villa Cicogna Mozzoni was born as a hunting lodge for the Mozzoni family in 1463. It was completed and embellished in 1559 with frescoes by the Campi brothers of Cremona and their school.

In the following century, Ascanio Mozzoni, a man of great culture, brought back from his travels the idea of setting the garden on seven levels. In fact, the most pleasing characteristic of the villa is its symbiosis with the garden. It is almost as though nature were invading the frescoed ceiling of the loggia with trails of vines and garlands of flowers. In 1580 Ascanio's daughter married Giovan Pietro Cicogna. The present owners descend from this couple.

The stairway of two ramps is to be admired. A stream runs between them and descends toward the reception rooms of the villa. There is a delightful panorama from the upper rooms of the house. The walled garden is a fine example of the formal Italian garden, with box hedges, basins, fountains, and a grotto providing a very interesting play of water. The rest of the grounds, rising up to the belvedere, are more naturalistic and romantic.

The apartments on the first floor are frescoed and furnished with paintings and furniture of various periods.

The garden reproduces the elegant, formal architecture of the sixteenth-century palazzo, softened by the fountains and the water that enlivens the landscape.
Following pages. The monumental stairway descends from the top of the hill and seems to flow directly into the rooms of the villa. The garden rises on seven levels, alternating from the formal to the landscape style typical of the romantic grounds.

Villa Cicogna Mozzoni

Villa Della Porta Bozzolo
Casalzuigno

Villa Della Porta Bozzolo was given to the FAI (Italian Environment Fund) in 1989. It is a typical Lombardy residence. The building was begun in 1500 in the form of a rustic lodge and then was gradually transformed into the family residence. However, in the first decades of 1700 the building achieved its present form, beautified by the grounds and the sumptuous decorations of the interiors. The rooms are, in fact, frescoed with floral ornaments in the rococo style. They give the whole a decorative airiness and harmony, and a vivacious relationship with the grandiose garden to the side of the villa.

The baroque garden is conceived as an infinite landscape, based on a longitudinal axis that actually starts outside the property and continues up to the hill of the belvedere. This rigidity, however, finds a breathing space in the large area known as the "theater," which is surrounded by cypress trees and a large fountain. This is a French garden that translates the spatial concept of the Italian Renaissance garden into great and theatrical dimensions; it maintains a rigorous geometry and makes artificial use of the water and the vegetation.

Furthermore, the huge park is based on a series of transversal axes that continuously create new perspectives; these are designed to be seen close up. Beside the grandiose architecture of the garden,

The baroque stairway connects the various levels of the garden along the sides of the hillside. In particular, it is an optical invitation to look along the visual axis that is theoretically infinite.

there was, in the past, also space for the cultivation of vines; an orchard of pears, apples, and peaches; and an outdoor lemon grove which was built in 1711 and re-modernized in 1724. Giuseppe Porta modeled it on the citrus groves of Lake Garda. The cypresses and the hedges were the only vegetation used as ornamentation. As one can still see, they were planted on either side of the "theater" and along the path that leads to the belvedere.

The unexpected glimpses of perspective and the theatrical effect of the descending terraces, crowded with statues, fountains, and balustrades, make this garden one of the most singular and fascinating of Italian garden architecture.

Above. One of the varieties of antique camellias that herald the arrival of spring.
Right. The calm, solid structure of the tree: lined avenue to the entrance of Villa della Porta Bozzolo reminds us that this property was originally a farm. In no way does the avenue of trees lead us to believe that beyond the walls there is a great baroque garden.

Villa del Balbianello
Lenno

Villa del Balbianello should be approached from the water. This is where the visitor can get the best view of one of the most beautiful and majestic gardens of the Lario. Built by order of Cardinal Angelo Maria Durini at the end of the eighteenth century, the villa rises on top of a wooded promontory overlooking the lake. It is such a fascinating view that it has been immortalized by dozens of painters and engravers of the landscapes of the Lario.

The explorer Guido Monzino donated it to the FAI in 1988, and his hand can be seen in the property as it stands today. English and French furniture of the seventeenth and eighteenth centuries, Flemish wall hangings, Chinese terra-cotta pieces, African and pre-Colombian sculptures, and a vast collection of delicate paintings on glass embellish the interiors as well as a small museum where Monzino has displayed documents and objects collected during his numerous expeditions.

The real masterpiece, however, is the garden, which is built on terraces carved out of the rocks. It is characterized by romantic pathways and dominated by the elegant three-arched rock that is silhouetted against the sky at the highest point of the promontory, a place of "leisure and delight." Majestic plane trees, magnolias, ilex, perfumed cypresses, and wisteria accompany the antique

The belvedere terrace of Villa del Balbianello is situated on the rocks overlooking Lake Como. The balustrade is lined with urns and statues. Approaching from the lake, one is struck by the uniqueness of this late eighteenth-century jewel.

statues. And the visitor is delighted by cyclamens, rhododendrons, snowdrops, and flowering borders of azaleas.

A thick trelliswork of climbing plants covers the rough, cold walls of some of the pathways in order to maintain the sense of sweet harmony that characterizes the entire garden. With austere rigor, hedges of laurel and box define the lawns and all the other areas, in line with the most classic traditions of the eighteenth-century Italian garden. Owing to the rocky substrata and the harsh structure of the land, it has not been possible to make it into a true Italian garden. The Balbianello, however, is unique, and nearly eludes categorization altogether.

Above. A group of buildings and three arches on the top of the promontory dominate the whole garden as it overlooks the lake.
Right. Eighteenth-century inspiration for the sumptuous balustrade. Contemporary inspiration for the Ficus repens *that is tidily allowed to embrace the columns.*

Garden of Villa Manzoni
Brusuglio

A very particular gardener worked at Brusuglio. Everybody called him Don Lisander, but he was Alessandro Manzoni himself, and he would make a face when people described him as a great man of letters. He would probably have preferred to be called a botanist. The present Villa Manzoni was built in the seventeenth century by the Imbonati Counts. When Carlo Imbonati died he left the villa to Giulia Beccaria, his dear friend and the mother of Manzoni. Beccaria and Manzoni arrived there for the first time in 1807. From that time on, the poet divided his time between his house in Milan and Brusuglio, where he began the restoration of the villa and the garden. He supervised the work with unusual passion. He searched for new ornamental plants, asking friends to send him seeds from France. And he personally dedicated his time to the cultivation of hydrangeas, which were almost unknown in nineteenth-century Italy. He also encouraged the diffusion of robinia (*Robinia pseudacacia*), a tree with highly scented flowers and preferred by bees because of its rich nectar. The robinia is common all over Lombardy thanks to this author. Today the bees still plunder the robinias in the garden at Brusuglio and produce a clear and very sweet honey that is highly prized.

Manzoni planted chestnut trees, magnolias, plane trees, and

Part of the grounds of Villa Manzoni. The statues, the age-old trees, and the pruned shrubs were the setting for the literary activity of Alessandro Manzoni.

beech along the avenues where he used to walk with his friends Tommaso Grossi and Antonio Rosmini. The catalpa under which he wrote *Il Cinque Maggio* is still alive to this day. In 1813 he had a belvedere built on a small rise from which he could admire the Resegone and the other hills of the Lecchese.

The present owners, Count Giovanni Lanza di Mazzarino and his wife Lycia, of the family of the Marchesi Berlingeri, have continued to make their home a lively and hospitable place, and they contribute to making it famous all over the world.

This page and facing page. The grounds of Villa Manzoni recall the style of the old noble villas of Lombardy. They were restored according to the taste of the period and recovered their vital energy. Here species and varieties of trees that had just been introduced into Italy were planted. Today they represent a precious testimony to the interest in botany and the art of gardening at the beginning of the nineteenth century.

Villa Monastero
Varenna

On the shores of Lake Como, Villa Monastero today represents one of the most interesting Italian residences because of its eclectic style: the works carried out between the end of the nineteenth century and the beginning of the twentieth century have added functional and decorative elements without destroying the traces of the preceding uses of the building. It is now a villa and a garden of great scenic and symbolic value.

The garden faces the eastern shore of Lake Como on the strip of land that stretches from Varenna toward Fiumelatte. It is the result of centuries of work adapting the sides of the steep cliff to a scenic design.

The land has been terraced and now lends itself to a series of different framed views with some recurring elements, such as the lines of cypresses along the avenue leading to the villa, the cedars of Lebanon, or the evergreen hedges.

The exotic species of trees planted all over the garden are of particular interest, and are witness to the mild climate of the Varenna area. They include African and American palms, American aloe (*Agava americana*), yucca, dracena, citrus, and oleanders, and some botanical rarities such as *Erythea armata*, a palm with large silver leaves in the form of a fan.

The lush, exotic vegetation of agaves and palms that appear all over the garden is witness to the particularly mild climate of the area of Lake Como.

The architectural elements that decorate the grounds are just as varied. Balustrades, statues, temples, flower pots, decorated parapets, and fountains—as far as the coffee house at the extreme border of the garden toward Fiumelatte—all recall baroque, classical, and even Moorish styles.

The way all these elements have been used is fascinating. Avenues and stairways blend into the surrounding landscape, with the lake in the background. In some cases, the elements seem only to serve to indicate the perspective of the landscape, like the twisted columns on the balustrade at the lake.

The most highly prized piece in the decoration of the garden is the sculpted group of the *Clemency of Titus*, by the neo-classical artist Giovan Battista Comolli. It was brought here by Walter Kees at the end of the nineteenth century.

The grounds are of considerable interest for their historical value, the wealth of the plant species, and because they offer the visitor a relaxing visit.

Viewed from the lake, Villa Monastero and its grounds appear like a monument to the precise fashion of architecture and landscaping between the late nineteenth and early twentieth century. Following pages. Left. Two pairs of spiral-shaped columns guard the entrance to the villa from the lake. Right. A view of Lake Como from the lower part of the garden, decorated with beds of seasonal flowers.

Villa Monastero

Garden of Poiega
Negrar di Valpolicella

Count Antonio Rizzardi commissioned the architect Luigi Trezza to create a park in 1783. The idea was to reconcile the romantic landscapes with the rules of the great tradition of the Italian garden. This garden stands in the center of the vineyards of Poiega in Valpolicella, which is an area traditionally associated with the cultivation of vines and which has been appreciated for centuries for the quality of its wines. The Count's principal merit was to have immortalized Poiega as "the last of the Italian gardens, a veritable triumph of perspective." (Georgina Masson)

The park rises on three parallel levels. In a semicircular annex, an open-air theater was made in the vegetation. Proportionately perfect steps are cut into the box hedges and cypresses, while the niches of the amphitheater, containing statues of characters from Greek comedies and tragedies, are made in hornbeam *(Carpinus)*. From the theater, the lemon grove can be seen through a colonnade of perfectly pruned cypresses. The lemon trees face the parterre of box, a few steps above the little lake.

The top level of the garden contains a little stand of hornbeam, ilex, yew, maple, and windmill palm *(Trachycarpus fortunei)* that is populated with stone-carved animals made by Mattoni. Among

The austere beauty of the art of topiary in the garden at Poiega, a late eighteenth-century tribute to the Italian garden just before it fell out of favor. The architect Trezza managed to combine the rules of tradition with the innovations of the landscaping style that was to dominate the following century.

these trees, there suddenly appears an enchanting circular temple, with a cupola of greenery created from the hornbeams, and with squares opening onto the green between the statues. It is like an invitation to interrupt one's walk and pause in the enchanted coolness and quiet of this place, where the presiding spirits speak to us of the delightful balance between nature and cultivation.

Above. The branches of the avenue of trees curve to form a tunnel that leads the eye towards the entrance to the villa.
Right. A circular stone temple can be seen through the thick foliage of the trees on the upper level. It contains mythological statues in niches and the charming vault is formed by hornbeams that let in the light from the sky through the foliage.
Following pages. The gentle shapes and rounded corners of the box parterre and the spectacular green theater in the garden at Poiega.

Villa Novare Bertani
Arbizzano di Negrar

Villa Novare Bertani is a few miles from Verona, at Arbizzano, in the heart of Valpolicella. It is the headquarters of the prestigious Cantina Bertani, which is famed for the high quality of its wine. The building has an attic that is crowned with statues and pinnacles. It also includes a seventeenth-century cellar where one can admire casks that are more than 140 years old.

The villa was designed by the architect Cristofoli for the Fattoris. It was completed in 1759 by the new owners, the Mosconi Counts, who also began to develop the garden.

Within the vast enclosure and behind the villa, a great English-style park opens up with ancient plants, among which are some imposing examples of swamp cypress *(Taxodium)* that surround a small island and reflect elegantly in the charming lake that has the same shape, although reduced in size, as the nearby Lake Garda.

In the central part of the villa is the wonderful Salone delle Grazie. The frescoes were painted in 1767 by Valliani and Prospero Pesci. They represent the arts. On the ceiling is an allegory of the seasons.

During the course of its history, Villa Novare has offered hospitality to illustrious men of letters, including the romantic

The crisp, classical façade of Villa Novare Bertani seen from the garden. Together they are a splendid example of the style that was in fashion in the Veneto region in the middle of the eighteenth century.

poet Ippolito Pindemonte. He lived in this area from 1792 to 1807, until the death of his benefactress, Elisabetta Mosconi.
Pindemonte described the beauty of Novare in some of his works, among which is the "Dissertation on English Gardens" published in 1817 in *Le prose e poesie campestri (Country Prose and Poetry)*.

Above. A view of the romantic, picturesque style of the cottage by the lake.
Right. The beautiful foliage of a stand of swamp cypress (Taxodium distichum) *is reflected in the lake which has the same shape at that of Lake Garda.*

Villa Arvedi
Grezzana

The majestic, seventeenth-century Villa Arvedi was bought in 1824 by Giovanni Antonio Arvedi of Verona, and his descendents are still here today. It is situated along the decline of a hill and bordered above by the thick vegetation of ancient olive trees that frame and protect it from the wind.

The garden was laid out in 1650 by the sculptor and architect G. B. Bianchi, as an elegant and somber ornament for the building. The villa stands on a grass-covered terrace. The parterre is the dominating feature; it is characterized by refined designs in the form of double fans, which are unique in Italy. The parterre, consisting of box hedges that are more than a hundred years old, creates a wonderful sense of space that is in harmony with the façade beside it. The avenue leading to the villa's entrance is majestic and lined with carefully sculpted box in geometric forms.

Behind the villa there is the elegant baroque chapel of St. Carlo Borromeo, which was built at the end of the seventeenth century. A rare and fabulous view of the parterre and facing hills can be seen by looking from the chapel through the central salon of the villa and out of the main entrance.

The exuberant liveliness of the climbing roses, the flowering annuals at their feet and in the pots make an even greater contrast with the austere evergreen vegetation of the parterre beyond the railing.

Villa Arvedi

Left. A breathtaking view of the parterre at Villa Arvedi and the surrounding hills. The fan-shaped intaglio of the box has no equal in Italy.
Right. Earthenware pots of lemons decorate the space near the villa and break up the uniform green of the formal vegetation.

Left. A fresco represents the façade of the villa with its great parterre set in the hilly landscape.
Right. Aerial view showing the pattern of the box parterre punctuated by other examples of box pruned into cone shapes. It is a unique example of eighteenth-century elegance and perfectly preserved over the centuries.

Villa Trissino Marzotto
Trissino

The property is formed around a Roman ruin, dating back to 1001 A.D. The land was made into a garden in 1400, redefined in 1700 by Mattoni, and completed by Frigimelica and by the architect Dal Pozzo. The more than one hundred statues by Orazio Marinali and Giacomo Cassetti, and their assistants, date back to the first half of the eighteenth century, as do many of the trees. Two villas were built in the eighteenth century. The higher villa belongs to the Trissino, of the Riale branch. It was destroyed in a fire at the end of the eighteenth century and was later rebuilt in a different style. This, too, was destroyed by fire on June 13, 1841.

The grounds extend over fifty acres and the large wooded areas alternate with clearings and fields. Stands of trees and exemplary isolated trees, some of which are more than two hundred years old, mark the vertical dimension. They act as a connection with the Italian gardens that surround the villas, embracing them with hedges, terraces, flower beds, and avenues enriched with plants pruned according to the art of topiary.

The upper villa is flanked by a wide lawn decorated with statues, and is surrounded by portals and walls. Above this is the "riding school." From here one goes down the avenue of cedars

The tidy stretch of lawn, the positions of the statues, balustrades and staircases, and the octagonal fountain also surrounded by statues, are witness to the sense of space and the expressive power of this place. After the villa burned down, the vegetation was all that was left.

Villa Trissino Marzotto

Left. Age-old trees, like this one, are witness to the special relationship between agriculture and nature at Villa Trissino Marzotto. The most precious examples are tagged.
Above. Two of the one hundred beautiful eighteenth-century statues that contrast with the vegetation.
Right. One of the spy-glass views. The parterre, and the tree-lined avenue, decorated with pots of citrus fruits, all lead the eye to the villa chapel.

that ends with Mattoni's parterre. In front of the lower villa is a double stairway that leads to the great octagonal fountain. The fountain is decorated with statues and contains fifty-three thousand cubic feet of water.

There are numerous wrought iron gates in the garden, a testimony to the imagination and manual craftsmanship of the Venetian artisans of the eighteenth century. The entrance gate to the lower villa is now attributed to Frigimelica.

In 1950 the entire property was in a state of disrepair. It was bought by Count Giannino Marzotto, who provided for the consolidation and restoration of the upper villa (which is still inhabited), the properties, and the grounds.

Above and right. Two views of the great octagonal basin beside the terrace of the lower villa. It is a miracle of harmonious composition and enlarges the already wide space where precious statues attributed to Marinali and Cassetti stand.

Left. In the eighteenth century, marble bases were placed to receive the earthenware pots and vases containing citrus fruits during the summer months.
Right. A poetic glimpse showing the integration of recent vegetation into the ancient structure of the garden. The roses frame the opening that contains a beautifully made marble urn.

Giusti Garden
Verona

Agostino Giusti was a knight of the Republic of Venice and a Gentleman of the Grand Duchy of Tuscany. The garden was created at the end of 1400, but today it has the form that was laid out by Giusti in 1570. It was designed as the backdrop for Palazzo Giusti. Pre-existing land and terraces were used so that, by taking a preordained path, the city would gradually come into view.

In front of the sixteenth-century atrium of the villa there is a line of cypresses that rises up as far as a grotto of stalactites. The view from the belvedere is one of the most beautiful panoramas of the city of Verona.

In addition to the collection of flowers, important Roman archeological finds, and the monumental "Goethe's cypress," the garden maintains its original sixteenth-century structure with acoustic grottos, fountains, pergolas, Italian-style box trees, mythological statues, and a small ancient labyrinth.

Through the centuries, it has been visited by many illustrious people, including Cosimo de' Medici, the writer Joseph Addison, Emperor Joseph II, Goethe, Mozart, King Carlo Felice of Savoy, and the composer Gabriel Fauré. Together with the adjoining sixteenth-century palazzo, this garden forms part of a complex of great artistic interest and architectural and classical beauty.

The Italian garden is famous for its beauty, the originality of design, and the beautiful statues that appear in the center of each section. Every aspect is perfectly preserved.

Left. The stairway leading to a grotto dates to the mid-sixteenth century. An enormous mask, designed to be able to emit fire from its mouth, adorns the grotto, an architectural feature of the belvedere. Seen from the atrium of the palazzo, the avenue of cypress trees forms a spy-glass view of this scene.
Right. The old fashioned enchantment of a corner of the garden. A simple vine plays the role of the only vegetation that decorates the architecture.

Garden of Villa Malenchini
Carignano

This vast property, situated to the southwest of Parma, was established by the Marchesi Lampugnani at the end of the sixteenth century. It extends to the foothills of the Tuscany-Emilia border of the Apennines. The ceilings were decorated by Cesare Baglioni, an artist who worked at the court of the Farnesi and in the most prestigious great houses of Parma.

In the seventeenth century, the Lampugnani were succeeded by the Cervi family. Giuseppe Cervi (1663–1748) was a famous scientist and physician to Elisabetta Farnese and to King Philip V of Spain. The lateral buildings of the villa were built during Giuseppe's lifetime, as was the rococo structure of the main entrance and the balcony above it.

The property passed from one hand to another until Count Edilio Raggio bought it in 1895 and gave it to his daughter Lietta Fortunata, nicknamed Fortuny, who was married to Marquis Luigi Malenchini. She dedicated herself to the creation of the great romantic garden. She was influenced by the imported taste of Leinhart, head gardener to Empress Marie Louise of France.

A straight, one-mile-long avenue of small cypresses connects the sixteenth-century villa to the eighteenth/nineteenth-century

In the mists of the fall in the valley of the Po, the landscaped grounds of Villa Malenchini are at their most romantic. Wild nature and cultivated plants, country life and urban refinement, live together in harmony.

garden. The perspective continues with an avenue of tall box hedges, sculpted according to the laws of topiary—in round and square forms—and flanked by a double row of colorful flowers.

The grounds spread over thirty-seven acres and contain mainly native species of trees such as oak, hornbeam, ash, alder, chestnut, and linden. There are also, however, many imported ornamental plants such as plane, citrus, sofora, fir, and paulownia. Here and there one can discover improvements from the nineteenth and twentieth centuries, such as a family chapel, a spring in false stone, a neo-baroque nymphaeum, and a serpent-shaped lake with a pretty little castle on an island—a perfect reproduction of the fortress of Fontanellato.

Above. The façade of Villa Malenchini with the straight avenue of topiary forms between two wings of age-old trees.
Right. The winding topiary hedge picks out the nineteenth-century statues and disappears into the grounds. They become the human element in contrast to their natural surroundings.

Garden of Villa Malenchini

Above. Another glimpse of the autumnal grounds of Villa Malenchini.
Right. Low hedges are pruned according to the fashion of topiary. They rise as unusual elements, square based, and are surmounted by domes which soften the general severity.

Villa Pasolini dall'Onda
Imola

Traveling among the orchards, fields, and vineyards of Romagna, one stumbles upon the small but extremely refined eighteenth-century garden of Villa Pasolini dall'Onda. The garden is out of alignment with the severe façade of the building. The contrast between the calm surrounding countryside and the delicate embroidery of box hedges, sculpted into perfect geometrical forms, creates a magical and surreal atmosphere.

The property arose around a fifteenth-century watchtower. The tower was decorated in the eighteenth century and can still be admired today. Over the years, the property expanded to include a nobleman's country residence, a forest containing deer and pheasant, and a farm that even in the eighteenth century produced fruit (mainly apricots) and excellent wine.

Throughout the generations of the Pasolini dall'Onda family, there has been a desire to restore the buildings and especially to preserve and enlarge the garden. They have introduced improvements and plants according to the prevailing taste of each succeeding age. Maria Pasolini Ponti was a student of the history of Italian gardens as well as a well-known pedagogue. She lived toward the end of the nineteenth century, and created a parterre of antique, modern, and Bengala roses. She also planted a collection

The low hedges to the side of the façade of Villa Pasolini dall'Onda create a sort of embroidery that enriches the building and reminds one of its noble eighteenth-century origins.

of aromatic and colorful lavenders (*Lavandula angustifolia, L. officinalis, L. vera, L. spica*, and many others).

Many great historical Italian and European gardens are now isolated, frozen in time. They are museum pieces, uprooted from the places in which they were created. Here, however, the property has remained intact, showing that it is possible to integrate the countryside, dedicated to the activities of agriculture on one hand, and gardens for pleasure on the other. It is not surprising that the custodians of this miracle is the Pasolini dall'Onda family, who is also among the founder members of the Association of Historic Residences and of Italia Nostra.

Above. View of the countryside and the estate that contains the villa and its garden.
Right. The topiary garden at Villa Pasolini dall'Onda is perfectly proportioned, with the small square surface and the height of the hedges. Ornamental elements rise on pedestals.

Palazzo Fantini
Tredozio

Palazzo Fantini is the splendid result of a series of stratified buildings constructed over the centuries. The original structure dates back to the seventeenth century, but it was only during the middle of the eighteenth century that the palazzo took on its present form. The art nouveau decorations are, however, of the nineteenth century. The present owner is responsible for the faithful restoration of the stables; cellars; grain storage barns that were typical of the ancient noble estates; and two great courtyards.

The grounds and the Italian garden have been the envy of the northern European courts since the nineteenth century. The grounds include trees found in traditional Italian gardens: ilex, chestnuts, cedars of Lebanon, Atlantic or deodar cedars, holly, *Pinus niger*, oaks, larches, and lime trees. These provide the background for the borders of box; the lawns and the *Nymphaea*; the begonias; the beds of antique roses; and the borders of saxifrage or ornamental salvia, known as lamb's or rabbit's ears.

With a riot of multicolored flowers that are renewed every season, the Italian garden breaks up the austere repetition of the pruned box hedges.

Above. A view of summer flowers in bloom.
Right. One of the rich borders of mixed perennials in the garden at Palazzo Fantini. Salvia, artemesia, stachy, campanula, and other varieties form interwoven colored groups of great beauty.
Following pages. Left. A small round bed of seasonal flowers introduces color to the dense green of trees and shrubs.
Right. Detail of the care with which the garden is laid out. In the summer the ancient basin of the nymphaeum is surrounded by colored Impatiens that rise up above a low curtain of box.

Palazzo Fantini

Garden of Villa Seghetti Panichi, Castel di Lama

While walking in the garden at Villa Seghetti Panichi, one should stop in the center of the lawn in front of the house. Here is the enchantment of the green and soft valley below, crossed by the river Tronto that once divided the Marches from the Kingdom of the Two Sicilies. One's gaze then lifts to the surrounding hills, as far as the mountain range stretching from Vettore to Montagna dei Fiori (Flower Mountain) and, in the distance, to Gran Sasso and the turquoise strip of the Adriatic sea.

This is only one of the surprises of a place that, until the end of the nineteenth century, was only a spur of rock dominated by an ancient castle on the Lama Torrent, and completely bare of any trees. Then, in 1875, the owners decided to change it into a residence for vacations and hunting. Thus the romantic park, designed by the great German landscape artist Winter, was born. There is a surprise around every corner. There is a lake with an island and a statue in the center, an artificial grotto with stalactites, gazebos, a circular bird snare, and an eighteenth-century fountain with the likeness of a mysterious two-tailed siren carved in white stone.

Nor should the great variety of botanical species be forgotten. Some of them are typical of the Marches, such as red beech and oak. Among these trees is the so-called "cathedral," thus named for its

The lake with its little island is today just as they were when designed by the German gardener Winter, in the late nineteenth century.

great foliage and the hundreds of birds that nest in its branches. There are northern trees such as magnolias, ilex, and linden trees. Among the exotic plants are two old Ginkgo bilobas. There is a *Cykas revoluta*, of prehistoric origin, and a *Chamaecyparis lausoniana*. A large family of palms has been cultivated in this park: groups of European fan palm *(Chamearops humilis)* and *Washingtonia philiphera*, with their great cascades of oval fruit; *Brahea dulcis*; and *Cordyline australis*, together with a *Chamaerops excelsa*, at whose feet flower the white bells of *Yucca gloriosa* and two rare examples of *Yubaea spectabilis*.

The rustic bridge (above) and the garden near the villa. The water reflects the building and the palms that rise beside it.

Garden of Villa Seghetti Panichi

The atmosphere of Villa Seghetti Panichi is the epitome of landscape romanticism and the nineteenth-century taste for the exotic.

Villa Oliva Buonvisi
San Pancrazio

The villa of Ludovico di Buonvisi was built around the sixteenth century by the sculptor and architect Matteo Civitali. It is among the very few villas in the Lucchese with a loggia on two floors and with columns made from one single block of Matriaia stone.

When the Buonvisi family died out in the nineteenth century, the villa was passed to the Paolozzi family. It then became the property of the Oliva family, which reclaimed and restructured it.

The grounds to the south of the villa are on three levels. On the central level there is an avenue of cypresses, decorated with masks and architectural features. The avenue leads to the main entrance to the house and is flanked by hornbeams weaving parallel to it. On the same level is the "basin of waterfalls," with bas relief and statues in terra-cotta, and which is next to the coffee house, with a stone table and benches in the shade of ilex. On the upper level there are basins containing fish and jets of water. Here there are woods of ilex, a lemon grove, greenhouses containing ornamental plants, a tennis court, and many large trees that surround the lawns. On the lower level of the garden there used to be a riding track bounded by pear trees and a *hortus conclusus* (an enclosed inviolate garden). This has now been replaced by a plantation of eucalyptus.

The grounds contain a rich assembly of tall plants and shrubs:

The grandiose scene of the middle garden on the south face of Villa Oliva Bonvisi. Halfway up the straight avenue that leads to the entrance of the villa, there is a beautiful tunnel of hornbeam.

Villa Oliva Buonvisi

Gingko biloba, camphor, olive (*Olea fragrans*), Feijoa, *Citrus triptera*, cedar of Lebanon, *Calycanthus*, ilex, pomegranate, hawthorn, and fir. It is made even more beautiful by fountains, water cascades, sculptures, and architectural decorations.

The Buonvisi stables are of particular artistic value and they are also the subject of a strange legend. Buonvisi maintained that his stables were even more beautiful than a famous room in the royal palace at Versailles. Louis XIV, King of France, sent his ambassador to inspect them. When he arrived he found the walls of the stables lined with gold coins bearing the image of the Sun King. The ambassador had to recognize Buonvisi as the winner of this challenge.

Above. Statues and other ornaments in terra-cotta decorate the flowing water between the upper and the middle garden.
Right. The north face of the villa with the sixteenth-century loggia in Matraia stone.

Villa Grabau
San Pancrazio

Villa Grabau stands on the slopes of the Lucchesi hills. It is an admirable example of neoclassical architecture of the nineteenth century, although the original structure was built by the powerful Diodati family and dates back to the beginning of the sixteenth century. At the time, the grounds contained native species that are still present in small wooded areas, with majestic examples of oak, ilex, hornbeam, linden, wild maple, and wayfaring tree (*Viburnum lantana*). Mention must be made of the species "banana shrub" (*Michelia figo*) and *Quercus andleyensis*, a hybrid plant that, in the Lucchese, only grows on this site.

Traces of the art nouveau garden can be seen in the palm trees, among them date palms from the Canary Islands and a majestic *Washingtonia filifera*. The whole is harmonious and well-proportioned. The diverse landscaping styles that have been employed over the years are also complementary to one another.

The property was bought by the German banker Rodolfo Schwartze for his wife, Carolina Grabau, in 1868. By succession it has come into the possession of the present owners, Francesca and Federico Grabau.

The open-air theater in box is of considerable interest. It is approached by lateral stone steps. Above the building is the

The grounds are of great botanical interest. Many species and varieties of rare trees have grown to considerable proportions. The most representative examples are labeled.

Villa Grabau

Italian garden, which is given some interest by female statues in white marble. It is symmetrical in almost all its details, from the magnolias pruned into the shape of obelisks on the first terrace to the pots of lemons on the second terrace. The garden is enhanced by worthy bronze masks and grotesque statues. The lemon grove is among the best preserved in the whole of Tuscany and is still a rare collection of one hundred plants in their original pots. Every plant has its own position in the greenhouse—an antique numbering board provides for the disposition of each one in its earthenware container.

Above. During the summer the water's edge above the villa is decorated with the citrus collection in valuable antique vases.
Right. It is characterized by the formality of the terraces, which are bordered by tall hedges that separate the garden from the wooded hills of the Lucchese.

Garden Corsini al Prato
Florence

Around 1620, the Corsini bought the palazzo built by Bernardo Buontalenti in 1572—and all the surrounding land—from the Acciaioli family. In 1624 they commissioned the architect Gherardo Silvani to design the garden and beautify the façade with a loggia.

The designs of the parterre, with pruned box hedges not more than twenty inches high, according to the classical method used in the Renaissance, are enriched by the linear and undulating movement. The central perspective is emphasized by an avenue of statues that gradually increase in height toward the garden gate at the loggia of the palazzo. Various Mediterranean herbs brighten the design of the garden: thyme, santolina (lavender cotton), lavender, roses, cistus (rock roses). Their geometry hides the fact that the land is uneven.

Almost like a protection of their confines, new patches of green have grown up around this pristine nucleus, adapting to the growth of the city that surrounded the property. These enlargements took place toward the middle of the nineteenth century and emulated the taste of the period, thus giving the garden an atmosphere of the English style that produces lively chromatic contrasts, particularly in the fall. This landscape was

The splendid late Renaissance parterre of the Corsini al Prato garden. The box is almost at ground level. The motif combines curving forms and typical squared shapes.

completed by the design of hidden paths and lakes, basins, and ruins decorated with statues. After more than a century, the undergrowth of the tall and thick shrubs has turned into a labyrinth, protected by enormous shrubs of bilberry, ilex, and pines; acanthus picks out the pathways. Today the garden is sometimes used for popular events such as the Annual Artisan Show in May.

Above. The loggia of the palazzo is the focal point of the central avenue. On either side, low, pruned hedges separate the citrus vases or statues.
Right. The severely pruned hedges are a symbol of man's control of nature. They embrace the embroidery of the pale colored, scented Mediterranean herbs that give the scene its beauty.

The Corsini al Prato garden as it is today is the result of blending the rigid and formal classic form with the use of plants according to the freer schemes of the centuries that followed. The result is unique and offers a beautiful visual effect.

Garzoni Garden
Collodi

The Garzoni garden is situated along the Lucca-Pistoia-Florence road and, in the seventeenth century, it was on the borders between the Grand Duchy of Tuscany and the Republic of Lucca. It is an extraordinary example of seventeenth-century and baroque taste based on the concepts of movement and wonder. It was already documented in the sixteenth century, and in similar form, in a design dated 1633, is extremely rich with scenic and chromatic inventions, even though the garden itself is relatively small (approximately 492 by 656 feet). In 1652, Francesco Sbarra wrote a little poem entitled *The Splendors of Collodi*, describing in minute detail and with great elegance the ancient wonders of the garden that was commissioned by Romano Garzone, a man of wealth and cultivated aristocratic taste who lived in Lucca during the seventeenth century.

The baroque structure of the garden originated with great excavation works to transform the gradient of the hill into a geometric series of terraces. Due to an optical illusion, this can only be seen from above; from below it looks like a single soft slope.

The villa is known as the "villa of the hundred windows." It is fabulously beautiful and various. It seems that the author of Pinocchio, Carlo Lorenzini, whose alias was Collodi, learned to read and write in the immense kitchen. He was the grandson of the

Seen from above, the garden at Villa Garzoni appears in all its glory of exquisite baroque taste.

manager of the Garzoni estate. The parterre at the entrance was the first feature to be built. Previously it was paved. Now it takes on the form of a labyrinth, which was a dominating theme of the mannerist and baroque era. The stairway of water is guarded by the great allegorical statues of the lion of Tuscany and the panther of Lucca standing above the weirs. Together they connect and unify the scenic complex of the garden. In 1786, the last Romano Garzoni commissioned the Lucchese architect Ottaviano Diodati to work at Collodi. He renewed the water system, enriching the garden with fountains and cascades. He added new statues and new additions of

Above. A drawing of the garden showing a theatrical setting spread over more than an acre and encircled by buildings.
Right. Bizarre forms in terra-cotta decorate a corner with potted plants and are protected by majestic evergreens.

decorative vegetation to the parterre at the entrance. The fame of the Collodi estate spread throughout Europe. In 1793 the king of Poland, Stanislao, asked the Garzoni family for a plan of the complex and, in particular, for the original rococo structure situated behind the villa, which was designed by the great architect Filippo Juvarra.

The Collodi estate passed from the Garzoni family to various other families including the Parravicino, the Poschi-Meuron, the Giacomini, the Gardi, and the present owner, Enrico Preziosi.

Above. One of the many original baroque statues that have been preserved.
Right. The stairway at Villa Garzone is probably the symbol of the garden itself, a superb synthesis of invention, artifice, and drama.

Villa Geggiano
Pianella

The villa at Geggiano has been the property of the Bianchi Bandinelli family since 1527. It is three miles from the center of Siena, in one of the most enchanting landscapes of Italy. The villa and the adjoining garden—considered national monuments—date back to the thirteenth century. Visitors experience the atmosphere of an elegant eighteenth-century summer home, thanks to the furniture and the period decorations that have been carefully preserved. Indeed, the complex owes its present appearance to restoration undertaken between 1780 and 1790.

The garden is decorated with groups of age-old cypress trees, sculpted box hedges, and old lemon plants in pots. They enclose an open-air theater that is cut into the vegetation and which has two entrances to the wings. These are low walls in late baroque style that are decorated with statues. The vegetable garden is decorated with a terraced orchard and a fish pond from which there is a magnificent panorama toward the city of Siena.

Within the building there is a small, beautifully designed chapel which has recently been restored. The entrance gallery inside the villa is decorated with frescoes painted in 1790 by the Tyrolean artist Ignazio Moder. They represent variations of the twelve months of the year that were taken from prints by

The garden leading to Villa Geggiano is planted with beautiful flowers contained within low pruned hedges. In the background there is a stand of age-old cypress trees.

Bartolozzi from drawings by Zocchi. The furnishings and wall coverings in the original "Venetian rustic" have been preserved intact in some of the rooms: the Blue Room, Vittorio Alfieri's Room, the Green Sitting Room, and the Room of the Cardinal and the Gossip. The great archeologist Ranuccio Bianchi Bandinelli wrote many of his books in this villa, and Bernardo Bertolucci shot the scenes of his film *Stealing Beauty* in the garden.

Above. A glimpse of the 1790 frescoes in "Venetian rustic" style by Ignazio Moder.
Right. The airy horizontal setting is interrupted only by the cypress trees that characterize this austerely elegant garden. It matches the landscape of the Sienese hills in which it is embedded.

The quality of its ancient forms and details contributes to the charm of Villa Geggiano. The Moder frescoes, the statues, and the terra-cotta vases were a result of the remodeling of the villa in the late eighteenth century.

Garden of Villa Gamberaia
Settignano

This property is relatively small (about two and a half acres), but it is a concentration of architectural wisdom and landscaping from the seventeenth to twentieth centuries. There is a spectacular view from the hill outside the village of Settignano that overlooks the city of Florence and the valley of the Arno river.

The villa rose over the modest house where the sculptor Rossellini was born. The work was finished in 1610 and was inhabited by the Lapi family until it was sold to the Marchesi Capponi, who enlarged the garden and added statues and fountains to it. At the beginning of the last century it was purchased by a beautiful and eccentric Russian lady, Giovanna Ghyka, the wife of a Romanian prince and sister of the queen of Serbia. She enhanced the austere vegetation of evergreens with colorful roses and other flowers. She transformed the eighteenth-century Italian garden beside the villa into a radiant and ingenious pattern of empty spaces and filled in areas—one in which basins of water bordered by sculpted box constitute the parterre.

By its clever use of space, the harmony of the layout is a masterpiece. A majestic, grass-covered avenue of 742 feet is the longitudinal axis. It ends with a nympheum decorated with bas-relief, which is surrounded by old cypress trees to the north and

The Italian garden in front of the villa contains box hedges typical of the art of topiary. They enclose bright and unusual basins of water created at the beginning of the nineteenth century over the pre-existing classic parterres.

the valley that opens up to the south. The transversal axis is 345
feet. Where it crosses the main axis there is a cabinet decorated
with statues, a play of water, and four symmetrical flights of stairs.
They lead to two stands of old ilex and to the lemon garden with
bushes of peonies and espaliers of "Albértine" roses.

The garden has been an important reference in the work of two
contemporary landscape artists: the English Geoffrey Jellicoe, and
Pietro Porcinai, the son of a gardener at Villa Gamberaia.

In 1904 Edith Wharton wrote: "After walking in this garden,
one comes away with the impression of having spent more time
and of having discovered more horizons than one really has."

Above. Bird's-eye view of the famous Italian garden at Villa Gamberaia.
Right. A charming corner embodying the combination of artifice and nature that inspired the
great landscape artists of the time.

Above and right. The art of topiary is at its most impressive at Villa Gamberaia. It sculpts the landscape and creates volumes and perspectives of rare stylistic harmony.

Villa Reale
Marlia

For many generations, Villa Reale at Marlia has been the residence of noble families and patrons of the arts. Napoleon's sister, Princess Elisa Baciocchi, created this grandiose complex at the beginning of the nineteenth century. She united the already vast property of the Orsetti with other surrounding properties.

According to the taste of the time, Elisa Baciocchi Orsetti modernized the old Palazzo Orsetti. She paid special attention to the loggia in the front of the building, which serves as an entrance. She left the splendid eighteenth-century gardens mostly intact, including the open-air theater cut into the vegetation and the Avenue of the Camelias, which is of particular value for its numerous rare species.

After the fall of Napoleon, the Dukes of Parma and then the Grand Dukes of Tuscany came into possession of the villa. Then, with the unification of Italy, it passed into the hands of Vittorio Emanuele II. The king gave it to Prince Carlo di Borbone. Carlo was disinherited following his marriage to Penelope Smyth, who was not of noble birth. Carlo and his wife spent the rest of their lives at the villa and were buried in the chapel in the grounds. Their son, who was an eccentric and a religious fanatic, fell deep into debt and the villa was put up for sale.

The Count and Countess Pecci-Blunt, parents of the present

An example of the harmony of natural vegetation and cultivated forms in the grounds of Villa Reale at Marlia.

owners, bought the villa just in time to stop the destruction of the grounds. They commissioned the French architect Jacques Greber to restore the garden. They created woods, streams, and a lake that make a romantic and theatrical complement to the series of classical Italian gardens of the time of the Orsettis.

The Pecci-Blunt family has revived the tradition of generous hospitality in the villa. Among those who have lived in the villa were Niccolò Paganini, members of the royal family, and the American painter John Singer Sargent.

Above and right. Eighteenth-century statues enliven the formal rigor of the powerful shapes created out of the vegetation. Following pages. The lake was created in the nineteenth century. Another view from above the Orsetti garden.

La Scarzuola
Montegabbione

St. Francis of Assisi founded the Convent of the Scarzuola in 1218,
where he planted a laurel and a rose and where, according to
legend, a spring burst forth. This is still a place of great devotion.
The property takes its name from *scarza* (marsh reeds), with which
St. Francis built himself a hut. A chapel now occupies this
legendary site. It contains a fresco and one of the first portraits of
the saint in levitation.

In 1956 the convent complex was bought and restored by the
Milanese architect Tomaso Buzzi. From 1965 to 1981, beside the
convent, he designed and built his ideal city; it was conceived
like a theatrical complex with backstage, proscenium, and so on.
Buzzi's city contains seven theaters and culminates in an
acropolis, which is a mountain of buildings whose interiors are
empty. They are built of many compartments, like an anthill, with
a dense series of units jumbled together and superimposed or
mounted inside one another. For the visitor, it is like a voyage of
initiation between the sacred city (the old convent) and the
profane city of the buildings of the theater that are weighed down
with symbols, references, and quotations.

Buzzi's work can be described as neo-mannerist, with its
distorted architectural mouldings, the variety of rustic objects, the

*The neo-mannerist architecture at La Scarzuola is immersed in the wooded hills
of Montegabbione.*

intended disproportions, the monsters, and the green statues in the style of Archimboldo. Nor should the close ties to surrealism be ignored, with their dreamlike, sinuous, labyrinthine features. This sort of architectural itinerary of the soul, inspired by the *Dream of Polifilus*—a fundamental Renaissance text on gardens—is carried out today, after the designs of Buzzi himself, by his heir and present owner, Marco Solari.

Above and right. A perfect "constructed" garden, La Scarzuola is enchanting. The jumbled and distorted architecture competes with the cadenced curtain of cypress trees.

Two glimpses of Buzzi's ideal city. It was built over fifteen years in the second half of the twentieth century and based on five hundred years of architectural theory.

Castel Giuliano
Bracciano

The fascinating grounds of Castel Giuliano lie at the heart of a great estate at the foot of the Tolfa hills. This was an ancient Etruscan and Roman settlement that, from the sixteenth century, became the property of the Marchesi Patrizi. Then, after centuries of neglect—and thanks to long and accurate renovations—the owners decided to restore the grounds, the castle, and the family church to the glitter and splendor that had long been forgotten.

The visitor is immediately immersed in the luxuriant vegetation of this enchanted garden, which has been cared for with a mastery that is the result of informed botanical and landscaping research. Aromatic herbs and flowering shrubs grow below majestic examples of *Pinus pinea*, oaks, cedars of Lebanon, magnolias, and maples. With superb refinement of tones and colors, they accentuate the contrast between the natural vegetation and the plants cultivated for ornamentation.

The real specialty of this garden, however, is the roses—they have transformed Castel Giuliano into one of the most important Italian rose gardens. There are hundreds of antique roses, among which one particularly remembers the magnificent examples of Albértine Barbier (variety of 1821), Blue Magenta (1900), and Sweet Juliette, which was created in 1989 by the Englishman

A symphony of colors and rich textures enhance the mixed borders at Castel Giuliano. They highlight the collection of roses in the part of the garden nearest the castle.

Austin. He took nineteenth-century roses as a model but obtained the re-flowering properties of the modern rose. The roses climb up the old walls in extraordinary splendor. Many other shrub roses form borders and hedges and share space with myrtles, foxgloves, lavenders, and the blue California lilac *(Ceanothus)*.

At Castel Giuliano history meets with the present in the height of elegance, and poetry marries art in the garden. Everything works to a romantic design, from the drops of water decorating the lady's mantle (above), to the foxgloves that rise freely among the roses (right).

Left. The rose garden is carefully and lovingly tended by the owners, who have inherited this beautiful and historic place.
Right. Examples of the age-old Pinus pinea, *oak, maple, and magnolia link the cultivated vegetation in the grounds with the natural Mediterranean shrubbery that surrounds the property.*

San Liberato
Bracciano

It has taken ten long years of dedicated and creative work, and a constant dialogue with nature, for Count Donato Sanminiatelli, his wife Maria Odescalchi, and the great landscape artist Russell Page to give life to a dream, and to share it with garden lovers all over the world. In the spring of 1964, when Page first set foot in this place, he said: "I know no other garden that has the magic of San Liberato." He enthusiastically accepted the commission to make this corner of paradise even more magical.

This authentic botanical park includes species from all over the world: Canadian maple, Japanese cherry, and Persian *Liquidambra orientalis* and parrotia live together with camphor and *Liriodendron tulipfera* (tulip tree), which seems to catch fire in the fall. One part of the garden is dedicated to plants needing acid soil—collections of camellias, rhododendron, perfumed *Choysia ternate*, and black bamboo can be admired. San Liberato is also a vast gallery of multicolored roses around a fountain adorned with nymphs.

There is also a lovely Romanic church of the first century. It is surrounded by a wood of old chestnuts. Beside it is a fig tree and a cypress that is hundreds of years old. From here there is a wonderful view of the volcanic lake of Bracciano and the conical profile of the Rocca Romana.

Shapes and colors abound in the beautiful woods of San Liberato.

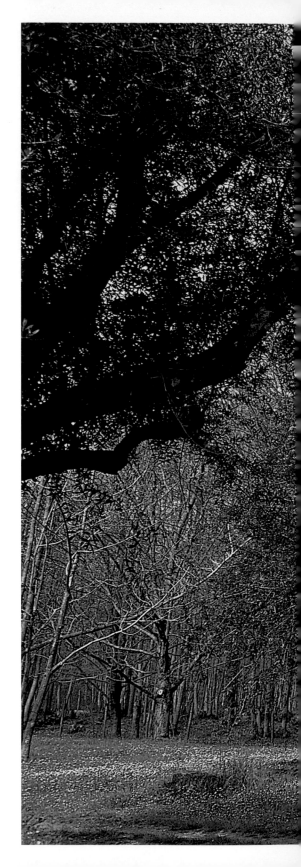

A taste of the exotic from the lush tropical garden (left) to the other kind of rarified symmetry (right) where the fountains, the terra-cotta jars, and stairways recall the classic Italian garden brought up to date.

Gardens of La Landriana
Tor San Lorenzo, Ardea

Along the littoral of Lazio, La Landriana is twenty-five miles south of Rome and spreads over more than twenty-five acres within a vast estate. It is a romantic place and full of fascinating surprises. It was bought in the 1950s by the family that still owns it. Designed by Russell Page, the gardens have been enlarged and modified over the years with the introduction of new collections of plants, among which are heather, hydrangea, antique roses, and camellias. This new work is due to the passionate curiosity and aesthetic sense of Lavinia Taverna.

The garden is divided into thirty "rooms." A thousand perfumed roses grow in the valley of the antique roses. Their beds are bordered by lavenders, thyme, and carnations. The roses also appear in an avenue of *Rosa mutabilis* and in another of "Bonica" roses; *Rosa banksiae* also decorate the walls of the old country construction. The pastel colors, the ghostly brightness of the white avenue, the silver of the olive garden, and the varying shades of the blue meadow flowers all give the visitor a great sense of peace and fulfilment.

A large part of La Landriana has managed to redefine the garden, in contemporary and Mediterranean terms, as a landscape or English garden. There are, however, some "rooms" that pick up

The lake can be seen from the thick woods at La Landriana. In front of it is the Valley of Antique Roses, spectacular in May and June with color and perfume.

the themes of the formal Italian garden. These include the Orange Garden, in which the strict geometrical design combines the perfectly regular round shapes of the little orange trees with the spheres of box at their feet.

The garden has been designed to flower throughout the year: narcissus, tulip, ornamental cherry, magnolia, and roses flower in the spring; plumbago, thorn apple (*datura*), passion flower, and hibiscus bloom in the summer; and camellia blooms in the fall. Every April, the gardens of La Landriana are the site of a prestigious national garden show.

Every one of the thirty "rooms" of the garden is a surprise and produces a new emotion. Nature apparently free to develop (above) and nature tamed (right, the Orange Garden with citrus and box pruned into obligatory shapes).

Above. The Italian garden.
Right. The "Spanish basin" – long and narrow with small pots repeated along the borders.

Castello di Vignanello
Vignanello

Vignanello is in the Viterbo area and probably contains the most elegant and celebrated Italian garden in the world. The property was formed around a tower built by Benedictine monks in 853 A.D., when this territory belonged to the Papal States. The first feudal lady, in 1531, was Beatrice Farnese. When she died, Pope Paul III confirmed that the inheritance should go to her daughter, Ortensia, married to Sforza Marescotti. The structure underwent changes conforming to the Ghibelline style of architecture of the time, designed by Sangallo.

The castle, as it is today, was designed in 1610 by order of Ottavia Orsini, wife of Marcantonio Marescotti. Indeed, she was the daughter of the creator of the fascinating garden at Bomarzo. In 1704, the castle passed into the hands of the Ruspoli family and it is still the summer residence of their descendants.

The garden annexed to the castle contains one of the most celebrated parterre of the seventeenth century. The rectangular space is crossed in length and breadth by four avenues that outline twelve parterres of box—aligned, squared off, and compact—that enclose a great basin bordered by four arched balustrades. These plant sculptures, originally of salvia and rosemary, give the garden the clarity of an abstract geometric design.

The Italian garden near the castle of Vignanello. The seventeenth-century design is the most rigorous and complex example of this style.

Many stylistic changes have taken place. This was particularly true toward the end of the eighteenth century, when French ornamentation was fashionable. However, the garden has remained intact. Ottavia Orsini, the lady of the manor four hundred years ago, has left a trace of her love for this place in the form of her initials and those of her sons, Sforza and Galeazzo. Thus we can be sure of the date of the garden.

Above. View from the central seventeenth-century fountain towards the façade of the castle.
Right. The parterre of box hedges is superbly pruned into geometric squares and curves. It is bordered on two sides by tall trees.
Following pages. Vases of lemons, urns with small flowering plants, roses, and iris among the curves of box soften the austere Italian garden.

Oasi di Porto
Fiumicino

Oasi di Porto (oasis at the port) stands at the mouth of the Tiber, a few miles away from Rome, on the site where Trajan's Port once thrived. This place is unique for the strangeness of the landscape, the vegetation, and its cultural history.

The center of Oasi di Porto is a vast body of water in a hexagonal shape. It is very similar to the one built by Emperor Trajan as a link to the pre-existing port of Claudius and for the storage and movement of goods destined for the city of Rome. The so-called "Trajan's Lake" was built in the 1920s as a water basin with a complex system of canals that irrigated ten thousand acres of agricultural land. The basin has a surface of eighty-one acres and is fed by the waters of the Tiber through a collection canal and a locking system that regulates the flow of water.

Nowadays, the whole area of Oasi di Porto is an ideal habitat and a safe refuge for various species of aquatic birds, both local and migratory. The migratory birds come in the spring and fall, breaking their flight between the Mediterranean region and northern Europe, where they go to nest. Birdwatchers' positions have been made and, particularly in late fall and winter, one can see ducks, grebes, cormorants, herons, snipes, seagulls, and sea

The Oasi di Porto is a magnificent example of how well an area can be looked after in a combination of wild nature and cleverly tended cultivation, in the shadow of two thousand years of history.

swallows. But there are other birds that have reappeared recently, such as the black-winged stilt. In all, there are as many as 130 different species.

The grounds of the Oasi are immense, with monumental pines, plane trees, ilex, lindens, poplars, ashes, and many other species. It represents an area of pure air and greenery, of prime importance to the city of Rome, and is a harmonious synthesis between history and nature, with its function as a bridge between the city and the countryside. The consortium that manages Oasi di Porto organizes twice-weekly guided tours in horse carriages.

Water is the dominating theme of the countryside at Oasi di Porto. It is an irresistible lure for more than one hundred species of birds that depend on it for their survival.

From the dense vegetation of the park to the shade of many monumental trees, the paths always lead to the water, with its calm and vast expanse reflecting the sky.

Villa Tritone
Sorrento

Overlooking the famous Gulf of Sorrento there is a garden protected by a mullioned wall; it is the repository of many ancient presences. It is here that Agrippa Postumus, nephew of Augustus, built his home. He decorated it with rare marble from the most distant provinces of the Roman empire, and collected precious Greek and Egyptian works of art. Ovid came here with Giulia, and was witness to a disquieting event: the eruption of Vesuvius in 79 A.D. was followed by a huge tidal wave that covered the place first with water and then with oblivion until the Middle Ages.

Time stood still for more than a thousand years. Then in 1200 A.D., a closed convent was built on the ruins of the ancient residence. In 1558 the Saracens raped and killed the nuns and pillaged and burned the building. Later, it was rebuilt by Dominican fathers. It also became a place of pilgrimage for the poet Torquato Tasso, who wrote *Gerusalemme Liberata* (*Jerusalem Liberated*).

At the end of the nineteenth century, Baron Labonia from Calabria began work on the construction of a garden on the *roches grises*, the spur of tufa that sustains it. At the beginning of the twentieth century, the extravagant William Walford Astor added paths, the features of an enchanted garden, and a collection of

A warm Mediterranean atmosphere of light and shadows under one of the pergolas at Villa Tritone.

exotic plants that have acclimated well. Rare palms, cycads, centuries-old noline, monumental *Strelizia alba*, and an old specimen of *Encephalartos* live together with the ruins of the Roman villa and add a new harmony to a place that is already filled with historical and scenic allusions.

Benedetto Croce lived here from 1943 to 1945, during which time he wrote a diary of those troubled years, entitled *Quando l'Italia era tagliata in due (When Italy Was Cut in Half)*. With loving care, the present owners, Rita and Mariano Pane, look after this heritage of art and nature.

Above. The interweaving of mild climatic plants creates a sublimely beautiful picture.
Right. The path across the rock garden of succulents leads to the two arches that overlook the Gulf of Sorrento.

Villa Tritone

The precious archeological relics are ancient presences, remnants of history. The garden at Villa Tritone has the enchantment of places that live both the past and the present, nature and cultivation in superb harmony.

La Mortella
Forio d'Ischia

William Walton, one of the most important composers of the twentieth century, lived on the island of Ischia from 1949 until the year of his death, in 1983. La Mortella is the splendid garden that his wife Susana created at Zaro, one of the most beautiful places on the island.

The garden was designed by the great landscape artist Russell Page. It was extracted from stony ground of volcanic origin. Today it contains more than eight hundred species of both extraordinary and rare plants: *Cyathea dealbata, Cyathea cooperi,* and Australian tree fern *(Dicksonia antartica), Metrosideros excelsa, Geranium maderense, Dracena draco, Puya berteroniana, Beschorneria yuccoides, Alocasia macrorrhiza, Spathodea campanulata, Chorisia speciosa, Erythrina caffra, Gunnera manicata,* and several species of tropical palms. Among the numerous aquatic plants decorating the fountain and the other bodies of water, the most evident are *Victoria amazonica* and *Victoria regia,* and many tropical *Nymphaea.* Meanwhile, the camellias brighten the winter garden with their flowers. A *Sala Thai* (oriental garden) has been created at the highest point of the property. It has a wooden construction and a lake with lotus flowers.

One of the ponds created at La Mortella to enable the garden to live. The property sits on arid, volcanic rock that becomes an interesting feature of the landscape.

The museum houses a wonderful collection of photographs by the great photographer Cecil Beaton. In the acting room, there is a fantastic and very colorful theatre designed by Lele Luzzati. The William Walton Foundation organizes concerts on Saturdays and Sundays with the participation of young musicians from the Conservatory San Pietro a Majella, part of the Fiesole Music School, and the Accademia of Santa Cecilia.

Above. Lady Susana Walton in the garden that she created in collaboration with Russell Page. Right. The dry walls are inhabited by plants of every kind, and not only those species requiring a hot and dry climate like the aloe shown in the photograph.

Scenes of lush and exotic vegetation in the upper part of the garden. At the top of the property stands the Thai Room, decorated in oriental style with a typical construction in wood, on a lake of lotus flowers (above). In the lower part of the garden the water is tamed and guided, as designed by Russell Page, into narrow channels of Arab inspiration (right and following page).

Il Biviere
Lentini

The garden of the houses of Il Biviere, belonging to Scipione and Maria Carla Borghese, is the garden of myth. Legend has it that Hercules, son of Zeus, slew the Nemean lion and brought it here as a gift to Ceres, goddess of agriculture. Here he created a lake that was named after him, *Lacus Erculeus*. Over the centuries the name of the lake was changed, and the Arabs called it *Beverè*, meaning a drinking trough for animals and a breeding place for fish. The State Archives in Palermo houses the original document of the Edict of King Martin who, in 1392, conceded the fief of "Il Biviere di Lentini" to an ancestor of Don Scipione Borghese, the present owner. The lake, which was rich with plants and animals, was dried out in the 1930s to prevent malaria.

It was abandoned by fishermen and hunters, and the property on the lake fell into decay, surrounded only by stones and dust. Today, thanks to the love and passion of its inhabitants, it has become a unique and special Mediterranean garden.

The ancient port faces south, enclosed by great hand-carved stones. It has become a green and pleasant invitation to the main façade of the "Casa del Biviere." The jetties have been restored with great attention and taste, and present a collection of succulent plants that seem to form a gangway of greenery.

Intense Mediterranean aromas combine with the shapes of rare and exotic plants in a setting of incomparable fascination.

The visitor is immersed in the spaces of the garden, where harmony has the color of orange, the scent of jasmine, and the inspiration of those who, through the centuries, have loved this land. Luxuriant palms, azure jacaranda, the bright-yellow flowers of palo verde, and antique roses embracing many fine examples of yucca are some of the garden's treasures. An unusual leaning gum tree (*Xanthorrhea*) faces the chapel of St. Andrew.

If time has ever been justified in flying, here in these perfumes and colors, it could find a reason to pause and enjoy some intense moments of beauty and tranquility.

Above. The façade and terrace of Il Biviere.
Right. A few trees defy the sky among the extraordinary collection of succulents planted in the ancient restored quay.

Stylistic harmony is provided by the strikingly sculptured plants, or like the borders, here on the left, by contrasting and charming colors.

Grandi Giardini Italiani/Great Italian Gardens
Piazza Cavour, 6, 22060 Cabiate (Como)
Tel. 031-756211/756769 fax 031-756768
e-mail grandigiardini@tiscalinet.it
web site www.grandigiardini.it

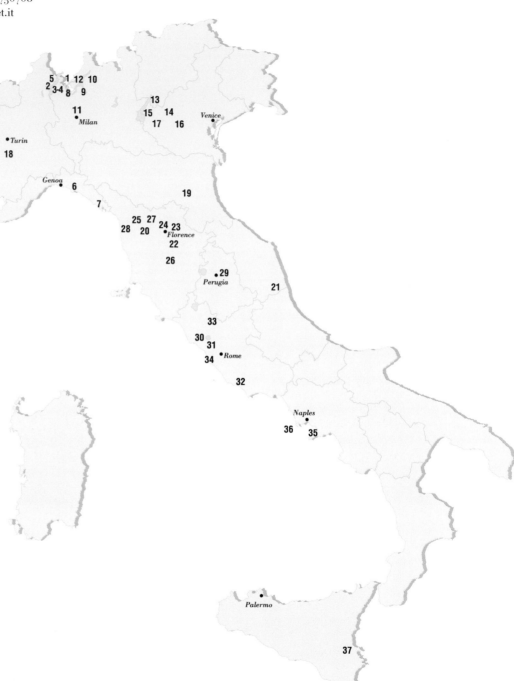

1. *Villa Favorita*, Lugano
2. *Grounds of Villa Pallavicino*, Stresa
3–4. *Borromeo Islands*, Verbania
5. *Botanical Gardens of Villa Taranto*, Verbania-Pallanza
6. *La Cervara*, Santa Margherita Ligure
7. *Villa Marigola*, San Terenzo Lerici
8. *Villa Cicogna Mozzoni*, Bisuschio
9. *Villa della Porta Bozzolo*, Casalzuigno
10. *Villa del Balbianello*, Lenno
11. *Garden of Villa Manzoni*, Brusuglio
12. *Villa Monastero*, Varenna
13. *Poiega Garden*, Negrar di Valpolicella
14. *Villa Novare Bertani*, Arbizzano di Negrar
15. *Villa Arvedi*, Grezzana
16. *Villa Trissino Marzotto*, Trissino
17. *Giusti del Giardino Garden*, Verona
18. *Villa Malenchini Garden*, Carignano
19. *Grounds of Villa Pasolini dall'Onda*, Imola
20. *Palazzo Fantini*, Tredozio
21. *Historical Grounds of Villa Seghetti Panichi*, Castel di Lama
22. *Villa Oliva Buonvisi*, San Pancrazio
23. *Villa Grabau*, San Pancrazio
24. *Corsini al Prato Garden*, Firenze
25. *Garzoni Garden*, Collodi
26. *Villa di Geggiano*, Pianella
27. *Garden of Villa Gamberaia*, Settignano
28. *Villa Reale*, Marlia
29. *La Scarzuola*, Montegabbione
30. *Castel Giuliano*, Bracciano
31. *San Liberato*, Bracciano
32. *Garden of La Landriana*, Tor San Lorenzo, Ardea
33. *Castello di Vignanello*, Vignanello
34. *Oasi di Porto*, Fiumicino
35. *Villa Tritone*, Sorrento
36. *La Mortella*, Forio d'Ischia
37. *Il Biviere*, Lentini

Addresses of Gardens

Villa Favorita
Castagnola Lugano, Switzerland
Owner: Baron Thyssen-Bornemisza
Tel: +41-91-9721741, fax: +41-91-9716151
Garden open from Good Friday to the end of October on Fridays,
Saturdays, and Sundays from 10 am to 5 pm.

Grounds of Villa Pallavicino
Stresa (Verbania)
Owner: Prince Domenico Pallavicino
Tel: +39-0323-31533 (office), and 0323-32407 (ticket office), fax: 0323-
934484
www.parcozoopallavicino.it
Open from March to November every day from 9 am to 6 pm. Guided
tours by appointment.
Le Scuderie Restaurant is open every day.

Borromeo Islands
Owners: Prince Borromeo
Isola Bella, 28838 Isola Bella (Verbania)
tel: +39-0323-30556, fax: 0323-30046
Open from March 24 to October 20, from 9 am to 12 noon and from 1:30
pm to 5:30 pm (5 pm in October)
Isola Madre (Verbania)
Tel: +39-0323-31261, fax: 0323-30045
Open from March 24 to October 20 from 9 am to 12 noon and from 1:30
pm to 5:30 pm (from 9:30 am to 12:30 pm and from 1:30 pm to 5 pm in
October).

Botanical Gardens of Villa Taranto
Via Vittorio Veneto 111, 28048 Verbania-Pallanza (VB)
Owner: Italian State, in care of Ente Giardini Botanici di Villa Taranto
(Public Corp. for Botanical Gardens of Villa Taranto)
Tel: +39-0323-404555, fax: 0323-556667
Open from April to October every day continuously from 8:30 am to 6:30 pm

La Cervara- Abbazia di San Girolamo al Monte di Portofino
(St.Jerome Abbey on Portofino promontory)
Via Cervara 10, 16038 Santa Margherita Ligure (Genova)
Owner: Enrico Mapelli
Tel: +39-0185-293139, fax: 0185-291270
www.cervara.it; e-mail: abbazia@cervara.it
For guided tours call 800-652110, or e-mail visite@cervara.it
Open March to October on first and third Sunday of the month by
appointment. Tours depart 10 am, 11 am, and 12 noon, all year round,
every day for groups of at least 30 people by appointment.

Villa Marigola
Viale Bigini, S. Terenzo Lerici (La Spezia)
Owner: Cassa di Risparmio di La Spezia
Tel: +39-0187-773549, fax 0187-773595
Open every day from 9:30 am to 12:30 pm and from 3 pm to 7 pm.
Guided tours for groups of at least 12 people by appointment.

Villa Cicogna Mozzoni
Piazza Cicogna 8, 21050 Bisuschio (Varese)
Owner: Cicogna Mozzoni family
Tel and fax: +39-0332-471134
www.villacicognamozzoni.it e-mail: eleopaa@tin.it
Open from April to October every day from 9:30 am to 12 noon and from
2:30 pm to 7 pm. Guided tours in Italian, German, French, and English
for groups of at least 20 people by appointment.

Villa Della Porta Bozzolo
Casalzuigno (Varese)
Owner: FAI-Fondo per l'Ambiente Italiano (Italian Environment Fund)
Tel: +39-0332-624136, fax: 0332-624748
Open from October to December every day from 10 am to 1 pm and from 2
pm to 5 pm (the grounds are open from 10 am to 5 pm).
Open from February to September every day from 10 am to 1 pm and
from 2 pm to 6 pm (grounds open from 10 am to 6 pm).

Villa del Balbianello

Lenno (Como)
Owner: FAI-fondo per l'Ambiente Italiano (Italian Environment Fund)
Tel: +39-0344-56110, fax: 0344-55575
Open from April to October every day except Mondays and Wednesdays, from 10 am to 12:30 pm and from 3:30 pm to 6:30 pm. Access from the lake to the villa is guaranteed by regular motorboat service from Lenno. Pedestrian access from Lenno (about 800 yards) is also allowed on Tuesdays, Saturdays, Sundays, and holidays.

Gardens of Villa Manzoni

Brusuglio di Cormano (Milano)
Owner: Marchese Pietro Berlingieri
Tel: +39-031-756211, fax: 031-756768
e-mail: grandigiardini@tiscalinet.it
Open by appointment only.

Villa Monastero

Varenna (Lecco)
Owner: Istituzione Villa Monastero, Provincia di Lecco (Villa Monastero Institute, Province of Lecco)
Corso Matteotti 3, 23900 Lecco
Tel: +39-0341-295450, fax: 0341-295463
www.villamonastero.it
Open from March 31 to November 3 every day from 9 am to 7 pm.

Villa Rizzardi, Poiega Garden

37024 Negrar di Valpolicella (Verona)
Owner: Contessa Guerrieri Rizzardi
Tel: +39-045-7210028 and 045-751940, fax: 045-7210704
Open from April to October on Tuesdays, Thursdays, and Saturdays from 3 pm to 7 pm. Wine tasting and guided tours by appointment, in English, German, and Italian.

Villa Novare Bertani

Località Novare, Arbizzano di Negrar (Verona)
Owners: Bertani family
Tel: +39-045-6011211, fax: 045-6011222
www.bertani.net
Open for visits to the villa, the garden, and the cellars all year round (except August and Christmas holidays) from 8:30 am to 12:30 am and from 3 pm to 6 pm.

Villa Arvedi

37023 Grezzana (Verona)
Owners: Arvedi family
Tel: +39-045-907045, fax: 045-908766
www.villaarvedi.it, e-mail arvedi@sis.it
Open for guided tours by appointment.

Villa Trissino Marzotto

Piazza Trissino 1, 36070 Trissino (Vicenza)
Owner: Count Giannino Marzotto
Tel: +39-0445-962029, fax: 0445-962090
Open for visits by appointment. The villa is closed on the second and third week of August and from December 20 to January 6.

Giusti del Giardino Garden

Owners: Countess Marina and Count Nicolò Giusti del Giardino
Via Giardino Giusti 2, 37129 Verona
Tel. and fax: +39-045-8034029
Open every day (except Christmas). In winter from 9 am to sunset and in summer from 9 am to 8 pm.

Villa Malenchini Garden

Strada Felino 2, 43010 Carignano (Parma)
Owner: Marchesi Malenchini
Tel: +39-0521-500019
Open by appointment only and for groups of not less than 6 people, from April 30 to November 15.

Grounds of Villa Pasolini dall'Onda

Via Montericco 10, Imola
Owner: Pasolini dall'Onda family
Tel: +39-0544-38583 and 335-7297264
Open from 9:30 am to 11:30 am and from 3:50 pm. Tours of the agricultural area and the vineyards is by appointment and for groups only, preferably on Saturdays.

Palazzo Fantini

Tredozio (Forli)
Owner: Gianfranco Fontane
Tel: +39-051-330095 and 0546-943926, fax: 051-332692
Tours of the garden and the museum of agricultural implements available on weekends and only by appointment.

Historical Grounds of Villa Seghetti Panichi

Castel di Lama (Ascoli Piceno)
Owner: Donna Giulia Pignatelli-Panichi
Tel: +39-0736-818621, fax: 0736-812493
www.marchesegrete.com; e-mail: marchesegrete@tiscalinet.it
Open every day from 10 am to 4 pm and at 4 pm for groups only and by appointment.

Villa Oliva-Buonvisi

55010 S. Pancrazio (Lucca)
Owner: Luisa Oliva
Tel: +39- 0583-406462, fax: 0583-406771
www.villaoliva.it; e-mail info@villaoliva.it
Open every day from March 15 to November 5 from 9:30 am to 12:30 pm and from 2 pm to 6 pm. Groups with appointment admitted when villa is closed.

Villa Grabau

Via di Matraia 269, 55020 San Pancrazio (Lucca)
Owner: ND Francesca and NH Federico Grabau
Tel. and fax: +39-0583-406098
Open from Easter to November 1 every day except Mondays and Tuesday mornings from 10 am to 1 pm and from 3 pm to 7 pm. During the rest of the year, open on Sundays from 11 am to 1 pm and from 2:30 pm to 5:30 pm, and every day for groups only by appointment. Closed Christmas and New Year's Day.

Corsini al Prato Garden

Via II Prato 58, 50123 Firenze (Florence)
Owner: Donna Giorgiana Corsini
Tel: +39-055-218994, fax: 055-268123
Open all year round by appointment only. Closed in August.

Garzoni Garden

Via Castello 1, 51014 Collodi (Pistoia)
Owner: Enrico Preziosi
Tel: +39-0572-429590
Open every day from April 1 to November 15 from 9 am to one hour before sunset. From 10 am in the winter months and on holidays and holiday eves. Other days visits can be arranged for groups by appointment.

Villa di Geggiano

Via Geggiano 1, 53010 Pianella (Siena)
Owner: Boscu Bianchi Bandinelli family
Tel: +39-0577-356879, fax: 0577-357075
Garden and the villa open for guided tours by appointment. Tasting of wine and home produce available on request.

Garden of Villa Gamberaia

Owner: Luigi Zalum
Via del Rossellini 72, Settignano (Firenze)
Tel: +39-055-697205 and 055-697090, fax: 055-697090
e-mail: villagam@tin.it
Visits to the garden open every day from 9 am to 7 pm. Visits to the villa by appointment only.

Villa Reale

55014 Marlia (Lucca)
Owners: Pecci-Blunt family
Tel: +39 0583-30108, fax: 0583-30009
e-mail: villareale@cln.it
Open from March 1 to November 30. By appointment only during other months. Closed Mondays if not holidays. Tours are always guided, with departures at 10 am, 11 am, 12 noon, 3 pm, 4 pm, 5 pm, and 6 pm.

La Scarzuola

05010 Montegabbione (Terni)

Owner: Marco Solari

Tel and fax +39-0763-837463

Open all year round by appointment. Guided tours for groups.

Castel Giuliano – Palazzo Patrizi

00062 Bracciano (Roma)

Owner: Marchese Patrizi Monitoro

Tel: +39-06-99802530, fax: 06-99809749

Open for group tours by appointment only.

San Liberato – Tenuta Sanminiatelli Odescalchi

Via Settevene Palo 33, 00062 Bracciano (Roma)

Owners: Sanminiatelli family

Tel: +39-06 9988343 and 06-99805460, fax: 06-99802506

e-mail: tenuta@sanliberato.it and info@sanliberato.it

Open from April to October on the first and last Sunday of the month from 4:30 pm; from November on the first and second Sunday of the month at 4:30 pm.

Gardens of La Landriana

Via Campo di Carne, 00040 Tor San Lorenzo – Ardea (Roma)

Owner: Heirs of Lavinia Taverna

Tel: +39-06-91014140, fax: 06-6872839

Open from April to October every weekend from 10 am to 12 noon and from 3 pm to 6 pm (from 4 pm to 7 pm in July and August). Every day for groups only by appointment.

Castello di Vignanello

01039 Vignanello (Viterbo)

Owners: Donna Claudia and Donna Giada Ruspali

Tel. and fax: +39-0761-755338

Open on Sundays by appointment only.

Oasi di Porto

Fiumicino (Roma)

Owner: Consorzio Oasi di Porto (Oasi di Porto Consortium)

Via Garibaldi 31, 00153 Roma

Tel: +39-06-5880880, fax: 06-5880885

Exclusive lunches in the dépendance on the lake can be organized for selected and limited groups.

Villa Tritone

Via Marina Grande 5, 80067 Sorrento (Napoli)

Owners: Rita and Mariano Pane

Tel: +39-06-6865152, fax: 06-6873796

Open all year round for groups only by appointment.

La Mortella

Via F. Calice 39, 80075, Forio d'Ischia (Napoli)

Owner: Lady Susana Walton

Tel: +39-081-986220, fax: 081-986237

www.ischia.it/mortella; e-mail mortella@pointel.it

Open from April to mid-November on Tuesdays, Thursdays, Saturdays, and Sundays from 9 am to 7 pm. Concerts on Saturdays and Sundays in April, June, September, and October.

Il Biviere

Contrada il Biviere, 96016 Lentini (Siracusa)

Owners: Princess Maria Carla Borghese

Tel: +39-095-7831449, fax: 095-7835575

Open by appointment only.

Photo Credits